ONIONS

Condiment :: Nutrient :: Medicine

OTHER BOOKS BY CLARENCE MEYER
Available from the Publisher

AMERICAN FOLK MEDICINE

THE HERBALIST ALMANAC 50 Year Anthology

MAKE YOUR OWN HERBAL RECIPES

OLD WAYS REDISCOVERED

SACHETS, POTPOURRI & INCENSE RECIPES

VEGETARIAN MEDICINES

ONIONS
Condiment :: Nutrient :: Medicine

Collected and Compiled by
CLARENCE MEYER

Edited by
DAVID C. MEYER

Meyerbooks, *Publisher*
GLENWOOD, ILLINOIS

ISBN 0-916638-16-2

Library of Congress Cataloguing-in-Publication Data

Meyer, Clarence.
    Onions : condiment, nutrient, medicine / collected and compiled by
Clarence Meyer ; edited by David C. Meyer.
        p.   cm.
    Includes bibliographical references and index.
    ISBN 0-916638-16-2 : $8.95
    1. Cookery (Onions).   2. Onions.   3. Onions—Therapeutic use.
I. Meyer, David, 1943-   . II. Title.
TX805.05M43   1993
641.6'525—dc20   92-32386
                                                                                CIP

*This book was designed by Dan Franklin
and typeset by Village Typographers, Inc. of Waterloo, Illinois.
Cover by Martin Hertzel Design.*

Meyerbooks, *Publisher*
P.O. Box 427
Glenwood, IL 60425

ACKNOWLEDGEMENTS

The editor is pleased to express his gratitude to Mrs. Marie Meyer, Nancy Henry Warny and Irene Richardson for their contributions to this book.

The publisher wishes to thank Mary Knickerbocker for carefully reading the manuscript and offering valuable suggestions and advice.

A portion of the material appearing in the "Onions in Your Garden" section originally appeared in Purdue University's Cooperative Extension Service Department of Horticulture publication *Onions And Their Relatives* by B. Rosie Lerner, Consumer Horticulture Specialist, and is reprinted with the permission of this organization.

The cover illustration was drawn by Clarence Meyer.

CONTENTS

ILLUSTRATIONS

ONION'S ORIGINS
AND FOLKLORE

❖ ❖

The Egyptians think it sin to root up or bite
Their leeks or onions which they serve with holy rite.
Sir Walter Raleigh

Wel loved he garleek, oynons, and eek lekes.
Chaucer, *Canterbury Tales*

One of the world's oldest records reveals that the Sumerians cultivated onions, leeks and garlic more than three thousand years ago. Onions were among offerings made to gods of the ancient Egyptians. Paintings and carvings on tombs and walls show onions on banquet tables of feasts. When the Egyptians built their awesome pyramids, they fed thousands of laborers with liberal amounts of onions, garlic and radishes to preserve the workers' health and strength, and also as a preventive measure against plagues. When Pharaohs were laid to rest in their massive tombs, they were well-provided with necessities, including medicines, for life in the hereafter. Mummies have been frequently found with onions affixed to various parts of the body which appear to indicate ailments suffered thousands of years ago. It is more than a remarkable coincidence that when onions are used medicinally today, they are employed in much the same ways as in ancient Egypt.

The common onion (*Allium cepa*) and its relatives— garlic, shallots, chives, leeks—are thought to be native to the Northern Hemisphere. There are more than four hundred species of Allium. They belong to the order of the Liliaceae, or lily tribe, and are bulbous plants, from which an acrid juice is obtained. They have similar properties and possess the same chemical constituents, although the degree of concentration of the juice varies greatly in different species, or even in the same plant, according to the country or latitude in which it has been raised. Plants grown in warm climates contain considerably more sugar. Bulbs grown in northern climates are stronger flavored and contain more tear-causing volatile oil, allyllpropyl disulphide. Onions are a source of vitamins A, B and C, and of calcium, phosphorus, potassium and trace elements.

The Greek term for onions was *Kromuon*. The word reflected the fact that the ancients were in the habit of closing their eyes to prevent the painful watering which often occurs when raw onions are peeled and handled. Garlic, which the Greeks held in abhorrence, was named *Scordium,* due to its disagreeable odor. Eschalots (or, strictly speaking, scallions) take their name from Ascalon, a town in Syria, near the Mediterranean, where the Greeks first procured them.

Allium cepa is the most widely used species in cookery as well as in domestic medicinal use. The Latin word *Allium* is thought to have originated from the rapid manner in which these plants grow. The Latin word *cepa* or *cepe* is thought to refer to the largeness of the head of the onion. The onion was also called *unio* because of its single root, without any of the offsets which most other bulbs have. From this word the English name "onion" is said to have been derived. The name "leek" is derived from the Saxon word *leac;* the plant was said to be an integral portion of the regular diet of the Saxon peasantry.

First introduced into the New World by way of the West Indies with the Spanish, the onion spread from there to all parts of the Americas. The onion was a staple of the early American colonists, and soon they introduced it to the native Indians.

Anything with a history as old and extensive as the

onion's will have myth and legend play a part in that history.

By the ancient Egyptians the onion was regarded as a plant partaking of a sacred character and as a symbol of the Universe. In the Egyptian cosmology the various spheres of hell, earth and heaven were concentric, like the layers of the onion skin. With them the onion was a common object of worship, and their veneration for this and other vegetables was ridiculed by the Roman satirist Juvenal (A.D. 60?-?140):

How Egypt, mad with superstition grown,
Makes gods of monsters, but too well is known:
'Tis mortal sin an Onion to devour,
Each clove of Garlic hath a sacred power;
Religious nation sure, and blest abodes,
When every garden is o'errun with gods!

Egyptian priests would abstain from the use of onions in food, probably as an assumption of austerity and a show of ascetic self-denial; and this led to the superstitious reverence with which the bulk of the people eventually regarded it. According to the Roman scholar Pliny the Elder (23-79 A.D.), "the onion and garlic are among the gods of Egypt, and by these they make their oaths." Thus much of the populace abstained from eating leeks, garlic or onions for fear of injuring their gods. Lucian, the Greek satirist and wit of the second century A.D., when giving an account of the different deities worshipped in Egypt, stated that the inhabitants of the ancient Egyptian city of Pelusium "adore the Onion."

But while many of the people did not dare to eat leeks, garlic or onions, others, including the laborers who built the pyramids, fed on them with enthusiasm. Another couplet by an unknown author sums up the zest of appetite, if not the religious zeal, which accompanied the consumption of the food of gods:

Such savoury deities must sure be good,
Which serve at once for worship and for food.

The onions of Egypt were also eaten and remembered with regretful longings by the discontented Israelites in the wilderness.

Mythologists relate that the Greek goddess Leto (called by the Romans Latona), who was the mother of Apollo, one of the most powerful of all Greek gods, lost her appetite during pregnancy and regained it by eating an onion. She thereafter adopted this vegetable and it was accordingly consecrated to her. Among the Greeks it would seem that the onion was considered symbolic of generation; it is told that the Athenian general Iphicrates, who married the daughter of the king of Thrace, received at his nuptials a jar of snow, a jar of lentils and a jar of onions, among other presents. Disciples of the Greek philosopher and mathematician Pythagoras abstained from eating onions, ostensibly because they grew during the waning moon, but probably because, like beans, they were considered too stimulating in their effects.

As with the Egyptians so, too, the English Druids regarded the onion as an emblem of the deity. In later times it was a custom for English girls to divine their future husbands by use of the onion. Barnabe Googe (1540-1594), the English poet, wrote:

> In these same days young wanton girls that meet for
>   marriage be
> Do search to know the names of them that shall their
>   husbands be;
> Four onions, five or eight they take, and make in every
>   one
> Such names as they do fancy most, and best to think
>   upon.
> Then near the chimney them they set, and that same
>   onion then
> That first doth sprout do surely bear the name of
>   their good man.

English country girls used to resort to a method of divination with an onion named after St. Thomas Aquinas. This they peeled and wrapped in a clean handkerchief. Then, placing it under their chins, they repeated the following:

> Good St. Thomas, do me right,
> And let my true lover come to-night,
> That I may see him in the face,
> And him in my fond arms embrace.

This verse was used in another ritual, intended for the same purpose. At the old holiday sports, a merry fellow who represented St. Thomas would dance in the firelight while the Yule log blazed, and give to the girls in the company an onion which they were to cut into quarters. Each girl then whispered to the onion the name of the young man from whom she awaited an offer of marriage, and, waving it overhead, she recited the above spell. If the young man happened to be present at this occasion, the onion became a rival to the Christmas mistletoe.

In the south of England a different form of this divination existed. When the onions were purchased the buyer would take care to go in by one door of the shop and come out by another. Obviously, a shop had to be selected which possessed two doors. The onions bought at such a shop were placed under the pillow on St. Thomas's Eve (December 29) and were sure to bring visions of one's true love and future husband. In some countries it was the custom to throw an onion after a bride, probably to ward off the Evil Eye and other powers of evil.

In other versions of these legends it was necessary for the damsel to be in bed by the stroke of midnight, and if the fates were kind, she would have a comforting vision of her wedding. Yet dreams in relation to onions were not always kind, as the following rhyme from an unknown source suggests:

To dream of eating onions means
Much strife in thy domestic scenes.
Secrets found out or else betrayed,
And many falsehoods made and said.

The leek was a food of the poor in the Orient: thus, it came to mean humility. It also became the emblem of

Wales, because it had the Cymric colors, green and white.

In the former kingdom of Bohemia (now a part of Czechoslovakia) the onion was used for fortune-telling. If hung in rooms where people congregated, the onion was thought to draw to itself the diseases that would otherwise fall upon those who inhabited the rooms. Garlic in Bohemia was given to dogs, cocks and ganders in the belief it made them fearless and strong.

In Arab and Chinese cultures, chives, like garlic and onions, protected against the Evil Eye, and warded off other misfortunes. All three were frequently tied over the doors of houses to prevent witchcraft. An onion hung in a door or window kept the devil away, as it was said to be respected by the devil on account of its being an object of worship like himself.

Garden advice, too, might fall into the realm of legend and lore when its practicality is suspect. Examples abound over the ages but we offer two passages only, from the pens of two men famous in their times. Pliny the Elder's *Natural History* was an encyclopedic account of the knowledge of his age. Pliny's work was chiefly a compilation; it is not reasonable to expect much original observation of nature from a man who was so devoted to books that it was recorded of him that he considered even a walk to be a waste of time! In his *Natural History* he was known to have mentioned indiscriminately any plant to which he found a reference in any previous book. Of the onion, he had this to report: "If you wish to have garlic and onions and such like not to smell and stink so as they do, the common opinion and rule is that they should not be set or sown but when the moon is under the earth, nor yet be gathered or

9

taken up but in her conjunctions with the sun, which is the change."

Though more worldly in his approach to the onion yet still more in the realm of lore than practical garden advice, Lord Bacon (1561-1626), the English philosopher and expert on all subjects, wrote: "If onions were taken up and allowed to dry for twenty days and then set again, they would increase in size, and still more so if the outer skins were taken off all over the bulb."

Onions also had a role in the prediction of weather and auguries of the mildness or harshness of seasons to come.

December twenty-fifth to January fifth—these twelve days are said to be the keys to the weather for the whole year. In France a superstitious practice on Christmas Day involved the laying out of twelve onions representing the twelve months of the year. Each onion was given a pinch of salt on the top. If the salt had melted by Epiphany, the month corresponding to the onion was put down as sure to be wet; but if the salt remained, the month was to be dry.

In rural cultures, when the onion's skin was thin and delicate, a mild winter was expected; but when the bulb was covered by a thick coat, this was held to foreshadow a severe season. An old farmer's saying stated:

Onion's skin very thin,
Mild winter's coming in.
Onion's skin thick and tough,
Coming winter cold and rough.

Obviously, the onion's uses and meanings are as varied as the cultures in which it has flourished.

GARDEN AND MARKET VARIETIES OF ONION

❖ ❖
❖ ❖

If Leekes you like
But do their smell dis-leeke
    Eat Onyuns
And you shall not smell the Leeke.

If you of Onyuns
Would the scent expelle
    Eat Garlicke,
And that shall drowne
    The Onyun's smelle.

Anonymous

Onion
A. cepa

COMMON ONION
Allium cepa

French: Oignon	*Spanish:* Cebolla
Italian: Cipolla	*German:* Zwiebel

Apparently a native of western Asia, the common onion was cultivated in ancient Egypt, India and Greece, and at an early date in China.

The form of the onion bulb ranges from flattened through globular to spindle-shaped. All the scales (that is, leaf bases) form complete layers, appearing as concentric rings in cross section. The outer scales are dry and papery, and consequently inedible. The inner scales are thick and fleshy. White, yellow and red varieties of onion are common; the color is in the dry scales and outer fleshy scales.

Two types have been developed, differing markedly in their propagation. One of these, known as top, Egyptian or perennial onion (var. *bulbellifera* Bailey), bears bulbets on the stalk. These occur instead of, or in addition to, flowers. Left to themselves the bulbets take root when the top falls over, or they may be separated for planting. (See the gardening section of this book for full instructions.) The second variety, known as multiplier onions (var. *multiplicans* Bailey), like garlic shows a marked tendency to divide within the outer scales into secondary bulbs which may be separated for planting. The common onion also may divide in the center and even subdivide, producing two or four sets of shoots on sprouting.

13

GARLIC
Allium sativum

French: Ail ordinaire   *Spanish:* Ajo
Italian: Aglio   *German:* Knoblauch

A native of temperate western Asia, garlic has been cultivated in Egypt and other Mediterranean countries since prehistoric times. It is today highly esteemed in southern Europe, although more as a condiment than a food. Garlic bulbs, held together by braiding the dry tops to form strings, are familiar sights in Italian markets. The bulb is compound, being made up of several easily separable, sickle-shaped, angular bulbs or "cloves." Thin, transparent, glistening scales of the primary bulb encircle the whole.

The crop is grown by separating the bulbs into cloves and planting like onion sets. The leaves are flat. In certain varieties, bulbets are produced among the flowers on the stalk as in top onions.

Racombole (*A. Schorodoprasum*) resembles garlic. It is grown chiefly in Europe, where it appears also to grow wild.

Garlic

A. sativum

Chinese Chives
A. odorum

CHINESE CHIVES
Allium odorum

This very unusual-appearing plant appears in early spring with refreshing green grass-like clumps. In summer its appearance changes when numerous stiff stalks, thirty or more inches high, rise from the clump. The tip of each stalk bears a bud which bursts forth with a dense umbel of starry white flowers. New flower stalks thicken the clump throughout the summer. New flowers also thicken each umbel. Bees love the long-lasting blooms.

Chinese chives have a delicate garlic-onion flavor and are rich in vitamin C and trace elements. The leaves, however, are not so succulent as those of the European species.

The minced fresh leaves are sprinkled over many native dishes in Asia, from Mongolia to the Philippines. Europeans use them to add a pleasant flavor to soups, salads, cheese or meat spreads. The fresh leaves, which are best in the spring, may be used like common chives, but are not recommended for use on sweet foods.

LEEK
Allium porrum

Although originally grown in Algeria and the Eastern Mediterranean and even in Switzerland, leeks are very adaptable and easily grown. In the Mediterranean region, where it appears to be native, the leek is grown from seed (not from sets) as a substitute for Spring onions. The blanched bases of the leaves, which form the edible portion, are somewhat swollen but do not form a pronounced bulb. As is true of garlic, the leaf blades are flat.

The bulb of a leek with a small part of its green has a delicate onion flavor that blends with many dishes. Raw leeks contain significant amounts of vitamin C as well as B vitamins, calcium, iron and trace elements. They are also a good source of potassium. As with other species of onions, leeks have a sulphurous oil and enzymes. All parts of the plant contain mucilage araban, pectin, fructose and saccharose.

The long, white stems are most commonly eaten. Leeks are used in cream of leek soup, consomme, stockpot, etc. The young fresh leaves of leeks are picked and eaten in early spring in Germany for "spring-fever" (Frühjahrs-müdigkeit). In France, blanched leeks are popular simply for braising, boiling, stewing, or steaming, and adding to melted butter, mayonnaise, sauces and meat stock. They can also be served in wilted-spinach salad. Leeks cooked in broths afford a mucilaginous and emollient ingredient for convalescent diets.

Leek
A. porrum

Welsh Onion
A. fistulosum

WELSH ONION
Allium fistulosum

The Welsh onion, also called the Welsh Bunching Onion, is actually a native of Siberia. Its name is said to be a corruption of the German word "welsche," meaning foreign, a term applied to the onion when it was first introduced into Europe during the late Middle Ages. It does not produce distinct bulbs, but the blanched lower portion of the leaves below the ground is somewhat swollen, tapering gradually to the green top. The mild, sweet bulbs, stalks and leaves may be eaten raw or used as a tangy addition to a salad.

Other names for this species are "Ciboule" and "Japanese Bunching Onion." This has been the principal garden onion in Japan and China since prehistoric times.

There is also a Perennial Welsh Onion (*A. lusitanicum*). While the first described variety (*A. fistulosum*) may be propagated from seeds as well as root divisions, the Perennial cannot be raised from seed as it produces none.

The Welsh onion is much more commonly used in the Orient than in the West.

Chives

A. schoenoprasum

CHIVES
Allium schoenoprasum

French: Civette *Spanish:* Cebollino
Italian: Cibollina *German:* Schnittlauch

Chives—the plural form is more commonly used than the singular—grow wild throughout Europe and in North America from New Brunswick and the Great Lakes to the Pacific and northward. This is a low growing evergreen perennial with bright upright leaves growing in dense tufts, making it a neat border or rock garden plant. The leaves are narrow-cylindrical and hollow, arising from small bulbs. In early spring chives produce bouquet-like clusters of rosy purple flower heads. The plant is a very prolific seeder.

Chives are cultivated for the mild-flavored leaves which are used for flavoring soups, sauces and various dishes. The succulent hollow leaves are best when freshly snipped. For fresh and tender leaves, trim the plant occasionally. Growing several clusters allows one to have fresh leaves available continually through the season. The minced leaves are sprinkled over cold or hot foods just before serving. Cooking destroys the flavor. When dehydrated, much of the flavor and nutritional value is lost.

Uses for minced fresh chives are varied. Sprinkle on cottage cheese, soft cheeses, sour cream, yogurt, eggs, omelettes, souffles. Use in herb butter, mayonnaise, sauces and gravies. Add to appetizers, snacks and sandwiches, tomato juice, vegetable juice mixtures, and salads of all kinds. Chives can also be added to soups, broth, consomme, cooked vegetables, meats, fish and baked potatoes.

Fresh chives are a rich source of vitamin C—they are said to contain 50 to 100 milligrams of vitamin C per one hundred grams of leaves. They also contain carotene, vitamin B_2, a sulphurous volatile oil, and a large quantity of sodium constituents, such as calcium, potassium, phosphorus and iron. Chives work as appetite and digestive stimulants.

The following listing, which is not intended to be all-inclusive, offers a sampling of onions commonly available, either as produce in grocery and farm markets or as seeds or "sets" from nurseries. A brief description of the onion, its flavor or character and its frequent use are given in most instances.

CIPOLLE

The name for this onion is said to be derived from an ancient Roman word for onion—*caepa*. This is a golden onion with a round, slightly flat shape. Cipolle onions are mild-flavored. They are often served stuffed and baked.

EGYPTIAN/WINTER ONION, TREE ONION, WALKING ONION, Etc.
Allium opa vivapavum

New, tender shoots of this onion are used like chives. The older stalks are good for flavoring soups and stews. Stalks should be removed from the pot after cooking. The small bulbils are seldom offered commercially because of their size, but these, too, are suitable for cooking.

HYBRID WHITE BERMUDA

A long-time favorite, these attractive onions are large, sweet and crisp. They hold together well and are most often used for frying as onion rings.

HYBRID YELLOW SWEET SPANISH ("FIESTA")

These onions have larger, more uniform bulbs with papery yellow skin which protects the crisp, fine-grained, white flesh. Many weigh a pound or more. They have small necks and a deep globe shape. They are mild and sweet with a "traditional" onion flavor. They keep well.

As its full-bodied flavor stands out in a rich broth, the "Fiesta" onion is often chosen for use in French onion soup. It is also excellent for deep-frying and for use in chili, tacos and enchiladas. It is often sliced on sandwiches and hamburgers, and is used frequently in green salads, coleslaw and potato salad. Fresh, minced "Fiesta" onion also may be sprinkled on many foods as a substitute for chives.

OSO SWEET

This new market variety is currently advertised by mail order as the only sweet onion available in winter. It is claimed to be sweeter than the famous Vidalia onion, thus the name OSO (oh so) Sweet. It is imported from the Andes mountains of South America and is available through the months of January and February.

RED SOUTHPORT

A popular mild, sweet and tasty globe-shaped onion with crisp, snowy-white flesh and deep red skin. It adds color and flavor to tossed salads and to marinated vegetable mixtures. The color and flavor last well in storage. Another variety with a similar taste is the California Wonder Red onion.

SHALLOTS
Allium ascalonicum

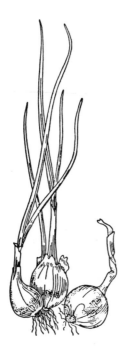

Shallots, sometimes called scallions, are a variety of the common onion. Horticultural authorities believe they originally came from Syria. They produce small pointed bulbs which separate similarly to garlic into cloves. These small bunching onions have a yellow or sometimes pink cast to the flesh. They have tall, upright green leaves and thick, cylindrical stalks. They are loved for their mild flavor and appetizing aroma.

Young shallots may be eaten whole. The bulbs are most popular in continental Europe and especially with French chefs. They are frequently used in sauces and herb butter, and with fish, marinades, meats, and fondue. They are also steeped in dill, tarragon and basil vinegars. Before the leaves from shallots dry, they are used as green onions.

TEXAS SWEET

An extra large onion with a papery yellow outer husk and firm, white flesh, this variety is grown in the Rio Grande Valley of Texas. With juicy, crisp texture, single centers, and sweet and mild flesh, these mild and flavorful onions are used in salads, casseroles and onion rings, or are grilled with seasoned butter.

VIDALIA

Vidalia onions have a typical flat, squatty shape with a creamy white interior. Grown in southeast Georgia, they are in season from May through July, although the supply often runs out before the demand lessens.

Vidalias are sweet, having the same sugar content as apples. The sweetness may vary from onion to onion. They are low in calories and high in vitamin C. Being tasty and crunchy—and, some say, lacking in the accompanying bad breath usually associated with onions—they are often eaten raw like apples. They are delicious sliced on a hamburger or chopped and added to coleslaw or potato salad; and also excellent when grilled or oven-roasted. Vidalia onions can be frozen, either whole or chopped, and used in soups, stews and other cooked dishes. It is best to use them where their flavor will stand out and be appreciated.

WALLA WALLA

Large and fragrant, these onions have flattened globe-shaped bulbs with yellow skin and white, crunchy flesh. Imported from France, they have been grown since the turn of the century in the Pacific Northwest. They are delicious whether eaten raw or cooked and have a sweet, mild and juicy flavor.

WONDER OF POMPEII

These small, round boiling onions are best used for pickling, although they are also used whole in stews and soups.

YELLOW SWEET SPANISH
AND JUMBO YELLOW SWEET SPANISH

Late-maturing and high-yielding onions of uniform size, they are large and globe-shaped, with light yellow skin and white flesh.

They are sweet, firm-textured and mild-flavored, store well and retain their flavor. They are considered all-purpose cooking onions.

Onions for the marketplace seem to be named for their color, shape, use, taste or origin. One will find red, green, white or yellow onions shaped like pears, torpedoes and globes. They are marketed as sandwich, hamburger or sweet onions, according to their predominate flavor and intended use. Slicer and odorless onions are promoted for their special qualities. A Spartan sleeper is declared to be "a perfect keeper" that won't spoil or soften. Rip Van Winkle is another onion developed for extended storage. Names that indicate an onion's origins, like Stuttgarter, White Bermuda or White Portugal, and local or proprietary names—Yellow Ebenezer, for example—tell little about an onion's best use. Often an identical variety of onion may be found to be marketed under a similar but not exactly the same name.

A wide and ever-changing variety of old favorites and new hybrid onions are offered every season. The above listing is but a hint of what one may find. (Countless varieties of onions are offered in European and Asian markets which do not appear in this country.) To be absolutely up-to-date on the onion plants currently available, write for catalogs from seed and nursery companies, which commonly advertise in popular magazines; or check your local market or nursery.

A listing of firms which commonly offer onion seeds and sets for planting will be found in Appendix E at the end of this book.

ONIONS
IN YOUR GARDEN

❖ ❖
❖ ❖

Onions are like an April day—
Good for the sad, good for the gay.
Excellent food and drug are they,
And oft we've used them either way.

Anonymous

CULTIVATION

Onions thrive under a wide variety of climatic and soil conditions. They do best, however, with an abundance of moisture and a temperate climate, without extremes of heat or cold through the growing season. In the South onions thrive in the fall, winter and spring. Farther north, winter temperatures may be too severe for certain types. In the North onions are primarily a spring, summer and fall crop.

SOIL PREPARATION

Onions will grow in almost any type of soil; a soil high in organic matter and well-drained is preferred. Add rotted manure, compost or other organic matter the fall preceding the spring crop and work into the soil.

Apply fertilizer that is high in phosphorus and potassium, such as 6-24-24, at four to five pounds per one hundred square feet of garden area in the absence of soil test recommendations. On high fertility soils, the fertilizer application should be limited to a side-dressing application of nitrogen two to three weeks after planting.

PLANTING

Plant onions as early as the soil is dry enough to be worked in the spring, since light freezes do not injure them. Later crops can be started up to May 15, but early planting is advantageous for larger bulbs and better storing onions. Plantings for green onions can be made anytime during the growing season.

Onions may be planted from sets, seed or transplants. The choice depends upon cultivar, use and availability. Onion plants form bulbs in response to daylength and temperature. Thus, cultivars that were bred for good production in the South will not form bulbs under northern growing conditions and vice versa.

Sets are usually used to produce green onions, although allowing them to mature will produce dry bulbs. Sets are small dry onions, up to three-quarter inch in diameter. Onion plants grown from sets are more prone to bolting, and their mature bulbs do not store as well as those grown from seed or transplants. Larger sets will make smaller bulbs and are best suited for producing green onions. Small sized sets produce larger mature bulbs. Select sets that are firm and not yet sprouted. Sets are available in white, red, or brown (yellow), with white the most commonly used for green onions.

Growing onions from seed requires a long period to produce either green onions or dry bulbs, and generally this practice is not recommended for home gardeners unless the seeds are started early indoors. Many garden centers offer a small selection of onion transplants in early spring.

For green onions, place sets or transplants upright about one inch apart in a furrow one to one and one-half inches deep. If dry onions are desired, plant them one to two inches deep, but three to four inches apart. Some gardeners make one planting and then pull plants for green onions, leaving one plant every four inches for mature bulbs. Cover the sets or firm in transplants and water thoroughly.

SUMMER CARE

Cultivate at a shallow depth to control weeds, particularly during the early part of the growing season. Additional water during dry periods will ensure a good yield. Apply a two- to four-inch layer of mulch around the plants to suppress weed growth and conserve soil moisture.

Onions are extremely sensitive, according to a recent report by horticulturists. During thunderstorms the air contains excessive concentrations of a gas known as ozone, which is toxic to onions. The disorder is called "onion tipburn."

HARVESTING

Green onions may be pulled and eaten fresh at any time while they are young. As they develop stronger flavor with age, use green onions for cooking. Larger bulbs may be pulled at any time during the growing season for fresh use. Bunching onions usually are ready four to six weeks after planting sets.

Dry bulb onions are mature in three to five months, usually by late August or early September. When the necks are thoroughly dry, or about ninety-five percent of the tops have bent over, dry onions are ready for harvest. Do not force the tops over. Pull the onions and place them in shade to dry, which should take two to four weeks.

When the necks have dried and tightened, cut the tops off about an inch above the bulb. Place the bulbs in a well-ventilated container, such as a mesh bag or a slatted crate. Fill the bags half full and hang them on overhead hooks if possible. Fill the crates half full and stack them on cross-bars to allow good air circulation.

Store onions in a dry, well-ventilated area, such as an attic or unheated room. Ideal conditions are thirty-two degrees Fahrenheit with a relative humidity of seventy to seventy-five percent. Although home gardeners usually do not have such ideal storage conditions, most can satisfactorily keep onions for two to four months. Never store onions with potatoes. Onions take on moisture from the potatoes and decay rapidly.

Throughout the drying and storing period, discard any damaged onions and those that have thick necks. Be sure the necks are dry, since several disease organisms can cause decay during the storage period if the bulbs are not thoroughly dried.

SPROUTING

Sprouting is promoted by exposure to warm temperatures, so keep the bulbs as cool as possible without freezing. Farmers from earlier times kept onions and garlic from sprouting by dipping the heads in salt water. Present-day commercial onion growers use a chemical sprout inhibitor called maleic hydrazide (MH-30). MH-30 must be applied two to three weeks before digging, or at about the time fifty percent of the tops are bent over. Application must be made while the stems are still green, so the chemical can be translocated down into the bulb. Onions sprayed with MH-30 cannot be used for planting purposes the next year, because they will not sprout. In addition, MH-30 is not readily available in packages economical for the home grower. The best bet for home gardeners is to keep temperatures as cool as possible.

TREE ONION, EGYPTIAN ONION

The tree or Egyptian onion produces small bulblets or sets where flowers are normally produced in common onions. Gather the bulblets as they mature and plant immediately or store until early fall. If planted in the early fall and allowed to overwinter in the garden, the bulbs begin growth early in spring and can be pulled for an early supply of green onions. Most strains are quite winter hardy.

POTATO ONION, MULTIPLIER ONION

The potato or multiplier onion is usually planted in the early spring. Occasionally it will overwinter under mulched conditions in southern climates. The bulb contains several small shoots, each of which produces a moderately-sized bulb by fall. Each clump of onions is then dug and can be used fresh, or stored, or replanted the following spring.

SHALLOT

The shallot differs from the common onion in that its bulb divides into multiple sections as garlic does. Since shallots seldom form seed, they are propagated by individual divisions of the bulb. The plant is hardy in most areas, but best results are obtained if the clusters of bulbs are lifted at the end of the growing season, stored and replanted next season. Shallot bulbs are more delicate in flavor than most onions. Most shallots are used as green onions since the mature bulbs are small. In some areas, any green bunching onion is called a shallot, regardless of the species. But the true shallot is a different plant. Follow the cultural recommendations for other onions. An old European proverb for planting shallots advises to "Plant them on the shortest day, lift them on the longest day."

Welsh Onion, Japanese Bunching Onion

The Welsh onions never form rounded bulbs but only white scallions, often used in Oriental dishes. In Japan, this onion is often incorrectly called the Japanese leek. Follow cultural instructions for green onions.

Leeks

Leeks are grown for the enlarged leaf bases at the bottom of the thick stem. They have a mild flavor and are used as green onions since no bulbs are formed. Leeks are grown from seed or transplants; start seed indoors early to get a head start on the growing season. Cut off the seedling tops when they are eight inches tall and transplant them five inches apart in the garden. Mounding the soil up several inches around the plants will produce a larger, white, tender leaf base. Leeks can be harvested any time from green onion size to before killing frost.

Garlic

Garlic, requiring a long growing season, often does not grow well in northern gardens. Garlic produces a group of cloves that are encased in a sheath. Plant individual cloves one to two inches deep and five to six inches apart. Each bulb contains about ten cloves, but the larger, outer cloves produce the best garlic. Elephant Garlic is a larger, milder flavored variety which should be planted about ten inches apart. Follow the cultural directions for growing onions. When the tops dry down, the bulbs should be pulled, dried, tied into bunches and hung in a cool, well-ventilated place.

CHIVES

Chives is a hardy perennial plant grown for its leaves rather than bulbs. Young, tender chive leaves have a pleasant, delicate, onion-like flavor. You can pick and use them any time during the growing season. Blue flowers appear early in the season, making chives an attractive specimen for the vegetable, herb or flower garden.

Plant seeds or clump divisions, and care for them as you would onion seeds or sets. Since chives are perennial, plant them where you can leave them for more than one season. They will gradually grow too thick, so divide and reset them every three years. Chives planted near tomatoes, carrots or roses are said to repel aphids.

For a year-round supply, pot a few clumps in the fall to bring indoors, and handle them as other house plants. Chives will thrive in any good garden soil and can be raised with success in flower pots indoors in summer or winter. They make a nice addition to the kitchen window garden or on the sun porch and in this way are available for immediate use whenever a fresh bit of "greens" is called for.

ONIONS FOR ORNAMENTAL GARDENS

Some varieties of onions, not used for medicinal or culinary purposes, are very attractive for ornamental use in the garden. While the leaves of flowering onions, or alliums, will have a faint onion odor if crushed, many of the flowers are sweet and fragrant. The flowers of most alliums grow ball-like clusters on the ends of their plant stalks. Individual flowers of different species are more or less showy and formed in variant compactness as well as colors. They are long-lasting in cutting or border gardens and will spread rapidly in favorable conditions.

Most allium bulbs are planted in early to mid-spring, generally four to six inches deep and six to ten inches apart. The plants usually like full sun and grow best in rich, well-drained soil that is kept moist during the growing season. Plants may be divided in early summer if the clumps become too crowded.

Among the most colorful species are the following:

A. aflatunens. Native of Iran. The flower clusters form a four-inch lilac-purple ball. Stalks are commonly two to four feet high.

A. albopilosum. Native to northern Iran. It is easy to grow in hot sunny places. The flowers form eight- to ten-inch balls. Individual blooms are glossy silver-violet with a green eye. They flower in mid-summer and the flowers may be dried.

A. caeruleum. The blue allium is one of the few flowering onions with this color blossom. The flower clusters average two to five inches wide on stems one to two feet high. They appear in late spring and the tiny bulbils which appear inside the clusters may be used for propagation.

41

The flowers may be dried and used in decorative arrangements.

A. christophii. This perennial, known as Star of Persia, blooms in the late spring and early summer. It raises sturdy stems, usually twenty inches high, on which are borne eight- to twelve-inch clusters of up to eighty flowers. The lilac-colored blooms, which have a metallic sheen, can be used for fresh bouquets and also for dried arrangements.

A. flavum. Native of southern Europe from France to Greece. It is easy to grow in sunny places. A foot-high, slender growing species with round, not hollow leaves. The yellow bell-shaped flowers appear on two-feet-high stalks.

A. giganteum. Native of Iran, Afghanistan and Central Asia, it is commonly known as Giant Garlic. This variety blooms early. The immense six-inch red-purple flower balls top tall stalks sometimes reaching five feet high.

A. karataviense. A native of central Asia, it is sometimes called Turkestan Allium. This variety also blooms early. The lilac-pink flowers top stalks six inches high.

A. moly. Lily Leek, the common name of this decorative species, refers to its relationship to edible garden leeks, although seed companies sometimes offer it under the name Golden Garlic. The flowers bloom on stalks twelve to fourteen inches tall and appear in mid- to late May. They are attractive, three-inch-wide loose clusters of bright, star-shaped yellow flowers. The flat leaves resemble those of iris.

A. neapolitanum. Daffodil Garlic, as it is commonly

called, appears in mid-spring. The flower stalks are twelve to eighteen inches high and bear clusters of fragrant, star-shaped white flowers. This plant may also be grown in pots.

A. ostrowskianum. Also a native of central Asia, it is easily grown in a sunny spot. This dwarf variety has deep rose blooms and a subtle fragrance. Like chives, it is an excellent plant for the rock garden.

A. pulchellum. The small reddish violet flowers appear in loose heads.

A. purdoni. Another native of Asia, it has rushlike foliage that grows three to four inches high and is a good candidate for the rock garden. The cluster heads of violet-blue flowers appear in mid- to late summer.

A. ramosum album. Native of Siberia, growing on grassy slopes and in meadows. The fragrant white flowers bloom in late summer or early fall.

A. rosenbachianum. Also known as the Rosenbach Onion, this showy species grows two to four feet high, although the leaves are somewhat shorter than the flower stalks. Round clusters of pink-purple flowers appear in late spring. The individual flowers usually have a dark stripe within the center of each petal.

A. schoenoprasum. Native throughout Europe and known as chives, this very hardy plant with its early blooming rosy purple flowers is excellent for the rock garden.

A. tanguticum. A variety with bluish lilac-like flowers.

This is but a sampling of the many onions used as garden ornamentals. Once again, the best way to deter-

mine current availability is to check with your local nursery or the latest crop of nursery catalog offerings. A
listing of firms which commonly offer flowering onions for
planting may be found in Appendix E at the end of this
book.

ONION RECIPES USED IN FOLK MEDICINE AND PROFESSIONAL PRACTICE

❖ ❖

Doctors in Onions different virtues see:
Quoth Galen, they should never given be
To bilious men, with whom they disagree;
Yet for lymphatics deems them wholesome food.
Asclepias praises them in highest mood.
They aid the stomach, also causes to start
A handsome color in a hairless part;
Which, with them rubbed, you thus can soon repair
Your tonsure, and bring back fallen hair.

The School of Salernum

A Sure Cure for Pneumonia.

Take six to ten onions, according to size, and chop fine; put in a large spider over a hot fire; then add about the same quantity of rye meal, and vinegar enough to form a thick paste. In the meanwhile stir it thoroughly, letting it simmer five or ten minutes. Then put it in a cotton bag large enough to cover the lungs, and apply to the chest as hot as the patient can bear. When this gets cool apply another, and thus continue by reheating the poultices, and in a few hours the patient will be out of danger. This simple remedy has never failed to cure this too often fatal malady. Usually three or four applications will be sufficient.

Reference may be made to
    AARON R. GAY & CO.,
122 STATE STREET, -   BOSTON.

Printed handbill, mid-19th century

A NOTE TO THE READER

The medicinal and therapeutic uses which follow are not to be considered in any way a recommendation for using onions as curative agents. Naturally one should not attempt to self-medicate any serious or difficult condition as there may be various causes that may require a doctor's diagnosis and treatment. The descriptions and recipes given herein are more in the nature of former practices and in the light of herbal lore.

All recipes refer only to fresh onions, fresh juice of onions or roasted or boiled fresh onions. Recipes do *not* refer to extract or onion oil, nor to dehydrated onions.

Fresh raw onions contain bacteria-killing volatile oils. Onions stimulate digestive activity, help lower blood pressure and tend to increase the discharge of urine. Onions are helpful against constipation. Their abundant cellulose and fiber give intestines momentum.

The beneficial value of onions depends much on how the bulbs are prepared and applied. The roasted or boiled onion becomes sweeter as it loses much of its volatile oils and acrimony. The cooked onion is used mainly for its demulcent and emollient properties.

Scientists now know that the volatile vapors of onions or garlic kill bacteria, protozoa and even larger organisms such as yeast cells and eggs of certain lower animals.

Externally onions are used as a rubefacient and in poultices. Soviet scientists believe onion paste reduces infection and helps to heal wounds. In their experiments they put fresh ground onion paste into a glass dish with a diameter equal to that of the wound in order to concentrate and retain the vapors to the infection without having the paste coming in direct contact with the wound.

In Old England it was a custom to put sliced raw onions on a dish in a sickroom where there was contagious disease. The onions were replaced by fresh ones every hour or as soon as they turned color. The old onions were burned.

L. Candlin wrote in "Health From Herbs" magazine:

A cut onion draws all diseases to it. This is a belief of many people. In our family we were brought up never to use an onion after it had been cut and left uncooked. There may be something in this. About twenty years ago, during an outbreak of measles in the North of England, some teachers in a country school decided to test this out. They hung peeled and cut onions up in all but one of the classrooms, with the result that the children in those classes were immune, whereas the classroom without onions had 24 children go down with measles.

A recent news report stated that onions are still hung on doors in Cairo's slums where disease thrives because of poor sanitation.

ALCOHOL

The onion was long believed to specifically prevent the intoxicating effects of alcoholic drink, and to dispel its evil consequences.

W.T. Fernie, M.D., *Meals Medicinal*, 1905

To avoid drunkenness eat raw leeks.

Williams, *The Garden of Health*, 1633

BOILS

Poultices of boiled or roasted common onion applied to boils diminishes pain and helps promote suppuration.

B.H. Barton, F.L.S. and T. Castle, F.L.S., M.D.,
The British Flora Medica, 1877

BRONCHIAL

For bronchitis apply repeatedly over the chest a good-sized onion, beaten into a pulp, within a flannel bag, each application being for four hours.

Fernie, 1905

Onions finely chopped and roasted in lard should be applied to the chest overnight to adults for coughs, bronchial catarrh and asthma. This may also be applied to children with a bad cough.

August Rogler, *Krautersegen*, n.d.

BURNS AND SCALDS — MINOR

Thoroughly bruise a raw onion and a peeled potato into a pulp. Mix mixture with a good tablespoonful of salad oil, and apply it to the burn or scald, securing it over the part by a linen bandage.

W.T. Fernie, M.D., *Kitchen Physic*, 1901

The juice of shallots combined with honey, is said to be a useful application in burns.

Rev. G.A. Stuart, M.D., *Chinese Materia Medica*, 1911

CHOLESTEROL

Eating a carrot, onion or an average portion of cabbage every day can help control cholesterol levels in the body. The vegetables contain calcium pectate, a substance that binds bile acids and causes the body to use up extra cholesterol. Researchers estimate that daily cholesterol levels can be cut as much as ten to twenty percent.

U.S. Department of Agriculture

COLON

Onions increase digestive activity, hinder putrefying in the colon and work against colon ailments.

A. Rogler

The onion bulb increases the peristaltic action of the intestines and is thus prescribed in cases of obstruction. It is used also in jaundice, hemorrhoids and prolapsus ani.

D. Sanyal and R. Ghose, *Vegetable Drugs of India*, 1934

COMMON COLDS

A good strong cup of onion tea drunk hot before going to bed will cure any cold man ever had. Try it and see. Don't spit it out after the first taste! Drink it for your own good.

Recipe from W. Lyons, Burgettstown, Pennsylvania, circa 1977

A basin of onions boiled in milk and thickened with groats or flour and a dash of nutmeg added is one of the best remedies for combating a heavy cold. Eat it very hot and jump into bed.

English recipe

A whole onion eaten at bedtime will break a cold by next morning.

English recipe

Onions are mostly used as a decoction with sugar, honey or milk. The decoctions were given for obstinate coughs, asthma, phthisis, and other pulmonary complaints.
Head Cold: Snuff the juice of an onion into the nostrils.

Dr. Fr. Losch, *Krauterbuch*, 1924

Slice onions and add a little sugar on each piece and allow this to stand overnight. The juice works well against head colds and coughing.

A. Rogler

COUGHS

Cut onions fine, cover with sugar and allow to steep overnight. This produces a thick sweet juice. For a child, give a teaspoonful every hour. Adults take two teaspoonsful.

51

This also works well for phlegm congestion in the respiratory organs, dropsy and for intermittent fevers.

Peter Mertes, *500 Heilpflanzen*, 1936

CROUP

Cut onions into thin slices. Between and over them put brown sugar and let it dissolve. A teaspoonful of the syrup will produce instant relief.

John C. Gunn, M.D., *Gunn's New Domestic Physician*, 1864

DEMULCENT

The common onion reduced to pulp by boiling and used either as pulp or decoction has been found serviceable in many diseases of local or general irritation such as catarrh of the lungs, urethra, and bladder.

Barton and Castle, 1877

DYSPEPSIA

A delicate lady who suffered with this complaint and had tried many remedies without being benefitted was advised to eat a small portion of raw onion, three times a day before meals, which in a few months effected a permanent cure.

Gunn, 1864

EARS

The juice of onion dropped into the ear or applied upon cotton was used in home practice for deafness. A small bulb, roasted and applied as hot as can be borne, is often beneficial in earache.

Barton and Castle, 1877

The core of a roasted onion relieves earache when introduced into the auditory canal.

Alfred Stille, M.D., LL.D., and John Maisch, Phar.D.,
The National Dispensatory, 1884

Cooked onions as warm as can be tolerated can be applied to relieve the pain of earache.

Mertes, 1936

If employed as a poultice for earache or for broken chilblains, the onion should be plainly roasted so as to modify its acrid oil. When there is running fetid discharge from the ear or when an abscess is first threatened with pain, heat and swelling, the hot poultice of roasted onion will be found very soothing and will do much to mitigate the pain.

Fernie, 1901

EYES

Onions cooked in milk and honey have been used as an eyewash.

Mertes, 1936

EXPECTORANT

Raw onions are occasionally taken with advantage as an expectorant by elderly persons affected with winter cough.

J. Pereira, M.D.,
The Elements of Materia Medica and Therapeutics, 1846

FEVER

In case of high fever take onions and slice them. Place them on the soles of the feet and they will draw out the fever. My little girl of two years old had a very high fever. I placed the onions in stockings on her feet. She went to sleep and slept for two hours and the fever was gone.

Letter from Mrs. R. Krummel, West Bend, Wisconsin, circa 1931

In malarial fevers onions eaten twice a day with two or three black peppers, give remarkable relief.

Eduardo Quisumbing, *Medicinal Plants of the Philippines,* 1951

A French army doctor treated grippe patients with juice from mashed onions by giving each patient, at the beginning of the disease, a quantity of two hundred cubic centimeters of onion juice in hot tea divided into three doses per day. The fever vanished in two days. Of eighty patients treated in this manner none died. One of the patients who refused to take this beverage developed bronchial pneumonia and was given the onion treatment by enema. The pain subsided in six days.

Maximino Martinez, *Plantas Medicinales De Mexico,* 1969

Medicinally the juice of shallots is rubbed on the body when feverish, especially for children. In the Gold Coast a

54

mixture of the bulbs with palm oil and large Capsicums heated in the sun is taken for fever.

J.M. Dalziel, M.D., B.Sc., F.L.S.,
The Useful Plants of West Tropical Africa, 1955

FLATULENCE

Eat daily three or four medium size mild flavored onions, raw or cooked.

Mertes, 1936

GASTRIC COMPLAINT

Eat an onion which has been steeped in brandy or whiskey.

Mertes, 1936

HAIR GROWTH

The juice of onions mixed with honey will not only cause the hair to grow and that effectually will even change the hair from grey to black provided it is regularly washed or bathed in the application.

H.V. Knagg, *Onions and Cress,* 1925

The onion juice anointed upon a bald head in the sun bringeth the haire again very speedily.

John Gerard, *The Herbal or Generall Historie of Plantes,* 1636

Onions steeped in the best French brandy with burdock roots are recommended for hair growth. Massage the fluid briskly into the scalp daily. Also rub a piece of onion upon the bare places.

Mertes, 1936

HEADACHE

Back about 1800, your ancestors treated their aching heads like hamburgers. They put a slice of raw onion on the forehead and a slice behind each ear. This was supposed to wipe out a headache and your forebears probably did get peace and quiet for their aching noggins by this means.

Undated news item

HIGH BLOOD PRESSURE

Take one large red onion, boil it in a pint of water, to one-half pint. Add this to one-half pint of whiskey. Take one teaspoon three times a day.

Undated letter from Mrs. C. Burwell

INHALANT

The fresh juice of onions is used like smelling salts for faintness in infantile convulsions, headache and epileptic and hysterical fits.

Dr. K.M. Nadkarni, *Indian Materia Medica*, n.d.

INSECT BITES

Vigorously rub raw onion on insect bites. This is especially helpful for bee and wasp stings. Rubbing raw onion also helps simple itching.

Mertes, 1936

KIDNEY AND BLADDER

The bulbs of onion cooked and mixed with coconut oil (olive oil or other vegetable oils may be used instead) are used in the form of an ointment applied to the abdomen to provoke excretion of urine.

Leon Guerrero, *Medicinal Uses of Philippine Plants*, 1921

Raw onions increase the flow of urine and promote free perspiration, insomuch that a diet of them with bread has many a time dispersed dropsical effusions caused by a chill, with arrested circulation in the kidneys, and skin surface.

Fernie, 1901

An infusion of leek seeds cleanses the bladder and the herb leaves are used for gravel pains.

Mertes, 1936

The juice works directly on the kidneys and brings forth the renal gravel and dissolves small kidney stones, but the juice should not be used for inflammation of the kidneys.

Hugo Hertwig, *Knaurs Heilpflanzen Buch*, 1954

LIVER

Captain B. Burch, of the District of Columbia, was afflicted with an abscess of the liver, deemed incurable by his physicians, and seeing some onions in his room, expressed a wish to eat one. Thinking his case desperate and no longer a matter of any consequence what he ate, his wife immediately gratified his appetite. After eating one or two onions he found himself much better, which induced him farther to indulge his appetite. He subsisted for several weeks entirely on onions, with only the addition of a little salt and bread; and from using this diet he was restored to perfect health, and is now a very hearty man in his fifty-third year. This, with innumerable instances of similar sort, ought to convince the young practitioner, that in the cure of this disease nature ought always to be consulted, as she seldom ever errs.

James Ewell, *The Medical Companion or Family Physician*, 1860

Nose Bleed

Nose bleed stops when one holds a fresh sliced onion under the nose.

Losch, 1924

Nutritive

The use of onions in the native diet is of considerable importance, as, although their protein and other content may be almost negligible, their value in accessory ingredients (vitamin B_1, etc.) is undoubted, and almost all people have from ancient times recognized their virtues.

Dalziel, 1955

It is a well-known fact that a Highlander, with a few raw onions in his pocket and a crust of bread or a bite of cake, can work or travel to an almost incredible extent—for two or three days together, without any other sort of food whatever. The French are aware of this; the soup a l'oignon is now universally in use after all late meetings and dances, etc., as the best of all restoratives.

Sir John Sinclair, Code of Health and Longevity
[as quoted from H.V. Knaggs, Onions And Cress]

PHLEGM (also see COUGHS)

A syrup made from the fresh juice of raw onions, with honey, is an excellent medicine for old persons troubled with phlegm in cold weather when air passages are stuffed and free breathing is hindered.

Fernie, 1901

PILES

For inflamed and protruding piles, the raw onion pulp of a bruised bulb will, if kept bound close against the part by a compress, and renewed as needed, afford certain relief.

Fernie, 1901

PNEUMONIA

Take six to ten onions, according to size, and chop fine; put in a large frying pan over a hot fire; then add about the same quantity of rye meal, and vinegar enough to form a thick paste. In the meanwhile stir it thoroughly, letting it simmer five to ten minutes. Then put it in a cotton bag large enough to cover the lungs, and apply to the chest as hot as the patient can bear. When this gets cool apply another, and thus continue by reheating the poultices, and in a few hours the patient will be out of danger. This simple remedy has never failed to cure this too often fatal malady. Usually three or four applications will be sufficient.

Aaron R. Gay and Co. (advertising flier), Boston, circa 1860

SCURVY

As onions can be kept over long periods, they were the stand-by for old-time sailing ships on long voyages for the prevention of the dreaded disease, scurvy. Sailors ate the onion raw in order to get full benefit of ascorbic acid.

Mixed with common salt the onions are a domestic remedy in colic and scurvy.

Quisumbing, 1951

SKIN PROBLEMS

Germans rub fresh sliced onions on corns. They also apply the bulb to itch, scabies and chilblains.

Mertes, 1936

SLEEP

Small onions eaten at night by those persons who are not prone to feverishness, will promote sleep, and induce a gentle perspiration.

Fernie, 1901

Onions eaten abundantly with meat causes one to sleep soundly.

Losch, 1924

Raw onions well mashed and inhaled for a few moments were believed to help nervous people to help induce sleep.

Old news item, undated

STINGS

A fresh slice of an onion applied promptly to part stung by a bee or wasp and changed several times generally gives relief. Irritation caused by stinging nettle plant may be relieved with raw onion juice.

J.D. Cromie, *Oxford Medical Adviser for the Home,* 1931

THROAT

William H. Crawford stated that while in Paris he was afflicted with a very sore throat, which did not yield to the usual remedies; he directed some onions to be beaten, and had them applied to the soles of his feet and legs, over which his stockings were drawn. The happy result was, that he had a good night's rest, and in the morning found his throat entirely cured. He communicated the cure wrought on himself to a French lady who was greatly distressed with a sore throat, which induced her to make the experiment, and the fortunate result was very remarkable.

Ewell, 1860

Spanish onion fried in lard and applied locally makes a splendid poultice. Roasted in coals it makes a good poultice for earache, toothache, sore throat, and sore chest.

The juice of fresh onions mixed with vinegar is useful in cases of sore throat.

Nadkarni, 1927

WHOOPING COUGH

Eat raw onions or onions boiled in milk.

Mertes, 1936

WORMS

Slice onions and add a little sugar on each piece and allow to stand overnight. The juice works well against worms in children.

Rogler

WOUNDS

A pork and onion poultice, good for wounds made by rusty tools and nails, bruises, and lacerated wounds: Take raw salt pork and about the same bulk in boiled onions. Chop together thoroughly fine in a wooden bowl. Apply warm and bind on about one-half-inch thick on the injured or wounded parts.

Prof. B.G. Jefferis, M.D., Ph.D., and J.L. Nichols, A.M.,
The Household Guide or Domestic Cyclopedia, 1905

In China the bruised bulb of fresh shallots is applied to wounds.

Rev. G.A. Stuart, *Chinese Materia Medica*, 1911

CULINARY USES

❖ ❖
❖ ❖

Let onion atoms lurk within the bowl
And, scarce suspected, animate the whole.
Rev. Sydney Smith

This is every cook's opinion,
No savoury dish without an onion:
But lest your kissing should be spoiled
Your onions must be thoroughly boiled.
Dean Swift

Onion recipes abound. Pick up almost any cookbook and unless it's devoted to a special ingredient, you are likely to find an assortment of recipes using onions. After all, many of our favorite recipes have onions as the main or sole ingredient. French fried onions, onion soup — anyone with even a mild familiarity with cooking can make a list of onion recipes. If you can't make a list of them, turn to any modern cookbook and you will find an assortment of onion recipes to choose from. And what would a book *about* onions be without a section of onion recipes?

In addition to several basic onion recipes, we have included favorite recipes offered by friends who happen to be excellent cooks. To complete this section we have gone back in time to see how previous generations used the onion and have found in old cookbooks some very interesting treatments of this favored food.

But first a few often-given hints for handling onions:

AVOIDING ONION ODOR AND TEARS

To reduce the pungency of onions, causing weeping eyes, try running cold water over the bulb while peeling. Chilling onions before slicing also reduces tears. (Other ideas are offered in Appendix C.)

To keep boiling onions from becoming offensive, boil a little vinegar in an uncovered pan on the stove.

When serving raw onions, soak in a teacup of milk for about one hour before serving, and they will lose most of their strong flavor. This milk can be used for white or cheese sauce later.

Onion odors may be removed from a knife by running it through a raw potato.

To remove onion odors from the hands, rub hands with a little celery salt before washing. Fresh lemon also removes odor of onions from the hands.

To remove onion breath, eat a few sprigs of parsley which have been dipped in salt or vinegar.

To remove the odor of onions from kettles in which they have been boiled, put some wood ashes, sal soda, potash or lye in the kettle, fill it with water and let it boil, then wash it in hot soap suds, and rinse well. Kettles in which fish have been boiled may be treated in the same way.

Old onions of any variety have a stronger flavor than the fresh bulb. When cooking old onions, start them in cold water so they will gradually be softened by the heat.

When storing cut onions in the refrigerator remember that milk, cream and butter absorb the aroma of cut onion, so keep the bulb in a glass container or plastic storage bag.

ONIONS ALONE

ONION SAUCE

3 to 4 white onions
½ pint milk
Butter size of ½ egg
Salt and pepper
A little cream

1 tablespoon flour, moistened
    with cold milk
Dust of nutmeg
Beaten yolk of an egg

Boil the onions until perfectly tender, then mince them fine, put the milk on the stove to boil, add the butter, season to taste and stir in the minced onions. When it begins to boil add the flour, moistened with cold milk (let it cream over boiling water). After the flour is well done add the cream and beaten yolk well mixed, also the dust of nutmeg; remove immediately and serve.

BOILED ONIONS

Onions of any kind
Butter size of an egg
1 tablespoon flour
Gravy
A little vinegar

Salt and pepper
Nutmeg
¼ cup cream
Beaten yolk of 1 egg

Peel the onions, cut them in pieces, unless they are small and preferred whole, boil them in salt water. If they are very strong change the water when about half done. When entirely done drain in a colander.

Dressing: Melt the butter, add the flour, mix well, and stir in enough hot water to make a creamy dressing, boil up once, then add rich meat gravy and a little vinegar, season to taste and add the onions, boil up once more, set back to simmer until wanted. Just before serving, add the egg and cream, beaten together.

FRIED ONION RINGS

2 huge Spanish onions should be enough for six people

Peel the onions. Slice ½ inch from each end and set aside for another occasion. Slice the central part of the onions about ⅛ inch thick, then push out the rings. Remove the smallest core part and put it with the ends. Now soak the rings in salted milk for about 20 minutes. Drain a few of them and shake them in a bag of seasoned flour. Deep-fry them until they are crisp and brown, then spread them out on absorbent paper towel and keep them warm while you fry the next batches.

Serve piled up on a warm plate, or as a garnish for meat or vegetables.

The onion rings can also be dipped in batter before they are fried (no need to soak them in milk first). This makes them heavier, more filling altogether, but they are good all the same.

ONION SALAD

The flavor of all the onion family is so pronounced that while a suggestion of it is valuable in nearly all salads, when used by themselves the flavor can only be subdued by the addition of seasonings. Slice tender young onions, potato onions or any kind at hand, into thin delicate slices. Season with salt, vinegar and red or black pepper. A French dressing is often used but most people consider the oil no improvement. Keep away from other people who have not also eaten of the onion. Toasted crackers are good with this salad.

SWEET ONION PIE

Pie crust:
1½ cups flour
½ teaspoon salt
½ cup chilled vegetable
  shortening
1 tablespoon butter
3 to 4 tablespoons ice water

Filling:
2 pounds thinly sliced Vidalia
  onions
½ cup (1 stick) unsalted
  butter
3 large eggs, beaten
1 cup sour cream
¼ teaspoon salt
½ teaspoon freshly ground
  pepper
Dash hot pepper sauce
Freshly grated parmesan
  cheese

For pie crust, mix flour and salt in large bowl. Cut in shortening and butter until mixture resembles coarse crumbs. Stir in water, 1 tablespoon at a time, just until mixture can be gathered into a ball. Wrap in plastic and refrigerate at least 30 minutes.

Roll dough between two sheets of floured wax paper into a large circle about ⅛ inch thick. Fit into a 9-inch pie pan; trim and flute edge. Refrigerate while you prepare filling.

Heat oven to 450 degrees. For filling, saute onions in butter in large skillet until crisp-tender. Remove from heat. Mix eggs and sour cream in large bowl. Stir in onion mixture, salt, pepper and hot pepper sauce. Pour mixture into prepared pie crust. Sprinkle with parmesan cheese.

Bake at 450 degrees 20 minutes. Reduce oven temperature to 325 degrees. Continue baking until top and crust are golden, about 20 more minutes. Cool on wire rack. Serve warm.

MARINATED VIDALIA SLICES

¼ cup red wine vinegar

¼ cup rice wine vinegar (or distilled white vinegar)

½ cup water

1½ teaspoons dill weed, fresh (chopped) or dry

1½ teaspoons dried basil

1½ teaspoons dried tarragon (optional)

1 clove garlic, minced

½ teaspoon light soy sauce

1 tablespoon olive oil (optional)

2 or 3 large Vidalia onions, peeled and sliced ½-inch thick

3 or 4 ripe tomatoes, cut in ½-inch slices (optional)

Combine all ingredients except onions and tomatoes, omitting oil if desired; blend well and set aside for flavors to merge at least 1 hour before using. Layer onion and tomato slices in flat ceramic dish; coat well with marinade, cover and chill. Makes 6 to 8 servings.

ONIONS AU GRATIN

2 large onions

Salt and pepper

3 ounces grated cheese

4 ounces bread crumbs

Pinch mixed herbs

1 ounce butter

Slice the onions and put a layer of them into the bottom of a well-greased pie dish. Sprinkle with pepper and salt. Add a layer of cheese and then a layer of bread crumbs. Repeat until all but one ounce of the cheese and one ounce of the bread crumbs are used up. Sprinkle the herbs over the last layer of onion and sprinkle over the remaining bread crumbs. Dot with butter and bake in a moderate oven for about an hour or until the onions are quite soft. Sprinkle with the remaining cheese and either return to the oven or put under a grill to brown. Serve hot.

BAKED ONIONS

1 large onion per person	½ to ¾ cup bread crumbs
1 bell pepper, minced	Salt and pepper
3 ounces cooked minced ham	2 tablespoons butter
2 cloves garlic, minced	1 egg, beaten
¼ cup parsley, chopped fine	

Preheat oven to 375 degrees.

Cut cone shape in each onion (peeled). Use extracted onion and chop finely, add ham, garlic, bell pepper, parsley, bread crumbs, salt and pepper. Combine with fork, the butter and beaten egg. (If mixture seems too dry add a tablespoon or two of oil.)

Stuff each onion with the mixture, arrange in a buttered ceramic/glass baking dish with lid, in one inch of broth or water, and bake covered for 30 minutes, then bake an additional 15 minutes uncovered.

ONION CUPS FOR VEGETABLES

Use number of onions as servings needed. Use large Bermuda or Vidalia onions.

Peel onions, cutting slice from each onion top. Cook onions in boiling water for 15 minutes or until tender but not mushy. Cool. Remove centers of onions, leaving outer shells intact. Spoon into onion shells any vegetables; for example, peas, beans cut small, broccoli floweret chopped, baby lima beans. Before serving heat in oven with pat of butter on top to warm vegetables. Cheese or white sauce can be poured over top if desired. Great for make ahead and buffet serving.

ONION CORNBREAD

2 cups chopped onion
¼ cup butter or margarine,
  melted
1½ cups self-rising cornmeal
2 tablespoons sugar
¼ teaspoon dillweed
1 (8-ounce) carton sour cream
Dash of hot sauce

1 cup shredded Cheddar
  cheese, divided
2 eggs, well beaten
¼ cup milk
¼ cup vegetable oil
1 (8¾ ounce) can of cream-
  style corn

Saute onion in butter until tender; set aside.

Combine cornmeal, sugar, and dillweed in a large bowl; add onion, ½ cup cheese, and remaining ingredients, stirring just until dry ingredients are moistened.

Spoon mixture into a greased 10-inch cast-iron skillet. Bake at 400 degrees for 20 minutes; sprinkle with remaining ½ cup cheese and bake an additional 5 minutes. Serves 8.

PICKLED ONIONS

(i)

3 quarts vinegar
6 pounds small onions or
  shallots
3 ounces turmeric

1 tablespoonful peppercorns
A few cloves
Piece of whole ginger

Peel the onions and put them into the vinegar to avoid discoloring. When all are done, fish them out and pack closely in bottles. Boil vinegar and spices 4 minutes and allow to get cold before pouring over the onions. The Stock Liquor (recipe follows) can be used instead of the above.

(ii) As the onions are peeled, put them into strong

brine, leave them all night, then remove them, dry between cloths and pack into jars.

To 1 quart of vinegar add 1 ounce each whole ginger and peppercorns and 1 saltspoonful mustard seeds. Boil 5 minutes, and when cold pour over the onions.

Stock Pickling Liquor:

3 gallons vinegar	1 teaspoonful alum
1 teacupful salt	1 pound whole pickling spice

Put the last three in a muslin bag and suspend it in the vinegar. Simmer gently for 5 minutes and store in a cask. May be poured over the vegetables cold, or heated to nearly boiling.

ONION VINEGAR

Two quarts of white wine vinegar, one tablespoonful of salt, two tablespoonfuls of granulated sugar, two pounds of peeled Spanish onions; grate the onions, mix them with the sugar and salt, allow to macerate for three hours, then pour over the vinegar; fill fruit jars ⅔ full, screw the lid on, shake well every day for a couple of weeks, then strain off through cheese cloth, fill into bottles and cork tight; this is very useful when a delicate onion flavor is desired with mayonnaise, salads, etc.

TO EXTRACT ONION JUICE

Cut a thin slice from one end of the onion, then press against a lemon grater, giving a slight rotary motion; turn the grater, and the juice will flow from one corner. Or, scrape the cut side with a sharp knife to secure fine pulp.

ONIONS BAKED IN HONEY

12 onions	⅓ cup butter
Salt and pepper	Powdered cloves
½ cup honey	

Precook the onions by boiling them until just tender. Place them in a buttered baking dish and sprinkle with salt and pepper. Heat the honey and butter together. Pour over onions, and sprinkle lightly with cloves. Bake until onions are golden brown.

SEVEN-ONION SOUP
(Served Hot or Cold)

1 large leek, chopped coarsely
2 medium yellow onions, chopped coarsely
3 medium red onions, chopped coarsely
1 large Spanish onion, chopped coarsely
1 large Vidalia onion, chopped coarsely
2 bunches green onions, chopped coarsely
2 cloves garlic, chopped coarsely
¼ cup olive oil
4 cups chicken stock
1 cup chopped Italian parsley
1 cup dry sherry
1 teaspoon salt
½ teaspoon black pepper
1 teaspoon poultry seasoning
1 teaspoon paprika
1½ cups half-and-half (or evaporated skim milk)
Sour cream or yogurt for garnish
Green onions, sliced fine, for garnish
Parsley sprigs for garnish
Paprika for garnish

Heat oil to 375 degrees in large skillet or wok. Add all the onions and stir-fry until limp, transparent and beginning to brown. Add stock, parsley, sherry, salt and pepper, poultry seasoning and paprika. Simmer, covered, for 1 hour, stirring every 15 minutes.

Strain broth and place solids in food processor or blender and puree. Return to broth and simmer 15 to 30 minutes, adjusting seasonings to taste. When ready to serve, add cream and heat through, but do not boil. Serve hot or chilled with a teaspoon of sour cream or yogurt in center of bowl, and sprinkle with parsley and paprika. Makes 10 1-cup servings.

ONIONS WITH ONE OTHER

ONION POTATO SOUP

4-6 medium yellow onions
6-8 medium sized boiling
   potatoes
¼ cup minced parsley
1 clove garlic, minced

1 teaspoon dried tarragon or 2
   tablespoons fresh tarragon
1 quart (6 cups) chicken broth
Roux

First make a roux with 3 tablespoons flour and 2 tablespoons of butter. Cook over low heat for several minutes; when the mixture begins to froth, reduce heat (do not let it burn). Add about 1 cup of broth, then add peeled sliced onion, potatoes, parsley and garlic; cook for a few minutes, then add remainder of broth and simmer for about 30-35 minutes. Before serving thicken with a little bit of butter which has been combined with tarragon.

BROILED TROUT WITH ONIONS

6 trout (½ pound each)
1½ teaspoons salt

½ cup cooking oil
3 raw onions

Clean trout and wipe dry. Season them inside with salt and brush outside with oil. Slice three raw onions and place inside trout in double layers.

Cut foil to individual size of trout and wrap separately in one thickness. Fold edges several times to seal. Fold ends until foil meets head and tail of trout.

Place trout on grill over charcoal and broil each side for 8 minutes. If trout weigh more than ½ pound, increase broiling time accordingly.

SWEET ONIONS WITH CREAMED PEAS

4 cups freshly shelled peas or 2
    packages (10 ounces each)
    frozen peas
2 teaspoons sugar
1 medium bunch of fresh
    chervil
1½ cups heavy cream

1 tablespoon unsalted butter
½ teaspoon salt
½ teaspoon freshly ground
    pepper
6 medium Vidalia onions (6
    ounces each)

In a medium saucepan, bring 3 cups of water to a boil. Add the peas, sugar and half of the chervil tied with string. Simmer the peas over moderately high heat until tender, 20 to 25 minutes for fresh and 3 for frozen. Drain the peas and discard the chervil.

Return the peas to the saucepan. Add the cream, butter, salt and pepper. Cook over low heat until the sauce is slightly thickened, 5 to 7 minutes; do not boil. (The recipe can be prepared ahead to this point.)

Cut a ¼-inch slice from the top of each onion and trim the root ends. Peel the onions and cut a cross in the root ends. Steam the onions, root-side down, until very tender, 25 to 30 minutes. Remove from the steamer.

Reheat the peas. When the onions are cool enough to handle, use a sharp knife to carve out a 2-inch deep core from the center of each one.

Finely chop the leaves from the remaining chervil sprigs. Place the onions in small bowls and fill with the creamed peas. Spoon the remaining peas around the onions and spoon the cream sauce on top. Sprinkle with the chopped chervil and serve hot. Serves 6.

RED ONION AND ORANGE SALAD

2 large red onions
2 large seedless oranges (or two ripe starfruit)
1 can (8-ounce) pitted black olives
1 bunch of watercress
1 small head Boston lettuce

Wash and dry gently the salad greens. Arrange on a platter (reserve a few sprigs of watercress for garnish). Alternate slices of red onion, oranges, add olives, watercress garnish, and dress with olive oil vinaigrette.

CUCUMBER AND ONION RELISH

1 large cucumber, washed, pared, chopped very fine
1 large onion, washed, peeled, chopped
1 tablespoon finely-cut parsley
1 tablespoon finely-cut chives
Tart French dressing, or oil and vinegar

Combine vegetables and herbs. Moisten with French dressing, or equal parts of oil and vinegar. Makes 1 cup.
Serve with baked oysters, meat loaf, or curried dishes.

CATSUP AND ONION RELISH
For Hot Barbecued Meats and Baked Spareribs

1 cup tomato catsup
½ cup finely-grated washed and peeled onion
¼ cup finely-chopped washed green pepper, seeds and fiber
   discarded
¼ cup finely-chopped stuffed olives
½ teaspoon dried oregano

Combine and mix all ingredients. Makes about 2 cups.

POTATO AND ONION CASSEROLE

Raw potatoes, chopped	Parsley, marjoram, thyme, sage
Onions, thinly sliced	Celery leaves, chopped
Salt and pepper	

Chop and drain raw potatoes, and thinly slice the onions. Place alternate layers of each in a well-buttered casserole. Sprinkle each layer lightly with salt and pepper, sage, parsley, thyme, chopped celery leaves, a bit of marjoram and dot with butter. Bake in a moderate oven until brown on top. Then carefully turn out upon a platter, dot with butter, and put under the broiler to brown on the bottom.

ONIONS AMONG OTHERS

ONION, TOMATO AND GOAT CHEESE TART

Preheat oven to 400 degrees.

Roll out pie pastry onto cookie sheet, cover with wax paper and rice (or pie weights) and bake for 10 minutes, till the crust turns a golden color. Remove from oven carefully, lift and discard wax paper.

Filling:
3 large onions sliced
3-4 large tomatoes seeded and sliced or 6-8 plum tomatoes
½ pound goat cheese
Garnish with black olive, minced basil/parsley, anchovies

Saute onions very gently in oil until onions turn soft — do not brown. Alternating onions and tomatoes, arrange on pastry, add crumbled goat cheese, favorite garnish, drizzle with some olive oil and bake in oven for 10 minutes.

BLACK-EYED PEA SKILLET DINNER

1 pound ground beef
1¼ cups chopped onion
1 cup chopped green pepper
2 cans (16-ounces each) black-eyed peas, drained
1 can (16-ounce) whole tomatoes, undrained and coarsely chopped
¾ teaspoon salt
½ teaspoon pepper

Cook ground beef, onion and green pepper over medium heat until beef is browned, stirring to crumble meat. Add remaining ingredients, bring to a boil, reduce heat and simmer 30 minutes, stirring often. Six servings.

BEEF EGGPLANT COMBO

1½ pounds ground beef
1 cup chopped onion
1 clove garlic, minced
1 can (16-ounce) tomatoes,
    cut up
2 teaspoons salt
1 teaspoon dried oregano leaves

½ teaspoon pepper
1 eggplant (1 pound) peeled
    and cubed (about 4½ cups)
1 cup quick-cooking rice
½ cup shredded mozzarella
    cheese

Cook beef, onion and garlic in large skillet until beef is browned. Drain off fat. Stir in tomatoes, salt, pepper, oregano, eggplant and 1 cup water. Heat to boil, stir in rice. Reduce heat and simmer covered about 25 minutes or until rice and eggplant are tender, stirring occasionally. Sprinkle with cheese. Cover and continue cooking until cheese is melted, 3 to 5 minutes. Serves six.

SWEDISH VEAL PAPRIKA

2½ pounds veal stew meat
2 large onions, chopped
2 tablespoons oil
2 teaspoons salt
½ teaspoon pepper
1 teaspoon paprika, more if
    desired

2 cups boiling water
2 tablespoons flour
¼ cup cold water
½ cup sour cream

Wipe veal and cut in 1-inch cubes. Saute onion in oil in heavy skillet. Add veal and brown lightly on all sides. Sprinkle with seasonings, add hot water, cover and simmer for 1½ hours. Mix flour and cold water to a paste, add to meat and stock and cook for 5 minutes to thicken gravy. Stir in sour cream and bring to boiling point. Serve at once. Six servings.

SWISS MEAT LOAF

2 pounds ground beef	1½ teaspoons salt
1½ cups diced Swiss (or Cheddar) cheese	½ teaspoon pepper
2 beaten eggs	1 teaspoon celery salt
½ cup chopped onion	½ teaspoon paprika
½ cup chopped green pepper	1½ cups milk
	1 cup dry bread crumbs

Mix all ingredients together in approximate order given. Press into one big greased loaf pan. Bake uncovered at 350 degrees for 1½ hours.

ONION, BACON AND POTATO SOUFFLE

¾ pound (2 medium) potatoes, peeled, quartered and boiled
2 teaspoons plus 1 tablespoon corn oil margarine
½ cup thinly sliced, chopped Canadian bacon
½ cup chopped onion
1 tablespoon flour
¾ cup skim milk
¼ teaspoon seasoned salt
Dash paprika
3 tablespoons grated Parmesan cheese, divided
1 medium egg yolk
1 tablespoon liquid egg substitute
2 tablespoons chopped fresh parsley
Vegetable cooking spray
3 medium egg whites, room temperature
⅛ teaspoon cream of tartar

Drain cooked potatoes thoroughly and mash with fork or in food processor. Set aside. Melt 1 teaspoon of the margarine in small skillet and cook Canadian bacon pieces 1 to 2 minutes. Add another teaspoon of margarine and stir in chopped onion, cooking 1 to 2 minutes or just until soft. Transfer bacon and onion to a small dish and set aside. To make the sauce, melt 1 tablespoon margarine in small saucepan, stir in flour and let bubble over low heat for 1 minute. Gradually whisk in skim milk and stir constantly until sauce bubbles and thickens. Remove from heat and add seasoned salt, a dash of paprika and 1 tablespoon of the Parmesan cheese. Beat in the mashed potatoes; add egg yolk, liquid egg substitute and parsley. Stir in reserved bacon pieces and onion; set aside.

Spray 3 2-cup individual souffle dishes (or 1 6-cup souffle dish) with vegetable cooking spray; wipe lightly with paper towel and sprinkle inside surface of dishes with remaining 2 tablespoons of Parmesan cheese. Set aside.

Place egg whites and cream of tartar in electric mixer bowl and beat on high speed until whites stand in soft peaks. Fold about 1 cup of the whites into the potato and sauce mixture to lighten, then gently blend mixture into whites until thoroughly combined.

Divide equally among prepared dishes and place in a baking pan with hot water ¾ the depth of the dishes. Bake in preheated 375-degree oven 25 to 30 minutes or until souffles puff 1 inch above the tops of dishes and are golden brown on top. Makes 3 2-cup servings.

APPENDIXES

❖ ❖

Appendix A
NUTRIENTS IN ONIONS
IN TERMS OF HOUSEHOLD MEASURES

	RAW ONION MATURE (2½″ dia.)	COOKED ONION (1 cup, 8 oz.)	YOUNG GREEN 6 small, no tops
Water (percent)	88	90	88
Food energy (calories)	50	80	25
Protein (grams) To build and repair all tissues. To help form antibodies to fight infection. To supply food energy.	2	2	Trace
Fat (grams) To supply a large amount of food energy in a small amount of food. To supply essential fatty acids.	Trace	Trace	Trace
Total carbohydrate (grams) To supply food energy. To help the body use other nutrients.	11	18	5
Calcium (milligrams) To help build bones and teeth. To help blood clot. To help the muscles and nerves react normally.	35	67	68
Iron (milligrams) To combine with protein to make hemoglobin, the red substance in the blood that carries oxygen to the cells.	0.6	1.0	0.4

continued*Appendixes*

	RAW ONION MATURE (2½″ dia.)	COOKED ONION (1 cup, 8 oz.)	YOUNG GREEN 6 small, no tops
Vitamin A value (int'l units) To help keep the skin and mucous membranes healthy and resistant to infection. To protect against night blindness.	60	110	30
Thiamine (milligrams) For normal appetite and digestion. For a healthy nervous system. To help change substances in food into energy for work and heat.	0.04	0.04	0.02
Riboflavin To help the cells use oxygen. To help keep vision clear. For smooth skin without scaling around mouth and nose or cracking at the corners of the mouth.	0.04	0.06	0.02
Niacin (milligrams)	0.2	0.4	0.1
Ascorbic acid (milligrams) To help cement body cells together and to strengthen the walls of the blood vessels. To help resist infection. To help in healing.	10	13	12

Onions, as with all other vegetables, do not contain cholesterol unless fats of animal origin are added. Vegetables usually contain less than one percent fat on a fresh weight basis.

Note: Several factors such as natural variation, differences in post harvest handling and storage, and variations in the processing and preparation method may cause a processed or prepared form of a vegetable to have a higher nutrient content than the unprocessed or unprepared form.

Source: The United States Department of Agriculture.

Appendix B
WILD ONIONS

There are many species of Allium which fall into the category of wild onion or wild garlic. All are similar in appearance, with a bulb at the base, leaves tubular or nearly flat, and flowers in a terminal cluster. All have a strong, penetrating odor.

Wild onions and garlic are found in North America over much of the United States and southern Canada. Some of the western states have nearly a dozen species growing within their borders. The following are examples of the more common wild onions:

The Nodding Wild Onion (*Allium cernuum*) is found on banks and hillsides from New York to South Carolina; west to Minnesota, South Dakota and New Mexico. In the northern part of its range, it may be found as far west as the Pacific Coast. The plant grows ten to twenty inches tall from an oblong bulb about half an inch in diameter or less, and nearly three times as high. The bulbs usually cluster. The leaves, all from the bulb, are very slender, channeled or nearly flat, and generally shorter than the flower stem. The rose-colored, or sometimes white, bell-shaped flowers form in a cluster on a stem which bends or nods. These appear in late summer. The bulb has a very strong flavor but, if parboiled, is said to be very tasty. A few of the leaves or the bulb may be used to flavor soups. The bulbs are also excellent for pickling.

The Swamp Onion (*Allium validum*) is found from Washington state to California, in moist places at higher altitudes, often growing in small beds. Although their bulbs are somewhat fibrous, they were acceptable in earlier times as a flavoring ingredient for soups or stews, when vegetables were difficult to procure.

Field or Wild Garlic (*Allium vineale*), a plant naturalized from Europe, ranges from Massachusetts south to Virginia and west to Missouri. The slender stem is clothed with the sheathing bases of the leaves halfway up the plant. The leaves are slender and channeled above; the flower cluster is often dense with small bulbs. This pasture pest favors moist meadows and fields. Dairy farmers hate it because it taints the flavor of milk and butter; wheat farmers fight it when it appears among their crops. Countless bulletins on its control and eradication have been issued by government and state agricultural stations. Wherever it appears, its presence will be noted in pastures, lawns, cultivated fields and gardens, and its odor or taste apparent in the hay, wheat, milk and meat which is produced in the area. It has been often written that "there is no weed worse than wild garlic and its complete eradication is devoutly to be wished. . . ."

Meadow Garlic (*Allium canadense*) is common from New Brunswick south to Florida and west to Minnesota, Colorado and Texas. This is the plant said to have fed Father Marquette and his men when they traveled from Green Bay, Wisconsin, to near the present site of Chicago in 1674.

(Material adapted from *Edible Wild Plants* by Oliver Perry Medsger and *Just Weeds* by Edwin Rollin Spencer.)

Appendix C
SUSPECT ADVICE

In cookbooks and other literature intended for the household, advice abounds concerning the handling and use of onions. Quite likely a book the size of this one could be compiled with the ingenious methods devised for avoiding the effect an onion has on the eyes while peeling it. To support this theory we offer several examples from a book titled *Household Hints* "selected from thousands of hints contributed by the readers to the women's pages of The Chicago Daily News." Published in 1933, this 224-page book recommends several ways to approach the enduring peeling problem:

- To prevent eyes from watering, hold a small piece of bread between the lips while peeling onions. Change to a fresh piece when it becomes moist.
- If matches are held between the teeth the sulphur tips will prevent eyes from smarting or watering when peeling onions or grating horseradish. The easiest way is to fold back the paper cover of a packet of pocket matches, such as men carry.
- Fewer tears will be shed in peeling onions if one sticks a piece of hard bread on the tip of the knife in peeling them.
- When preparing onions pour boiling water over them, let stand three minutes, then plunge in cold water one minute. Peel, slice or grind, they will not make your eyes water.

- Peel onions from the root and toward the sprout and avoid stinging eyes and tears.

For those who wish to employ onions for projects outside the kitchen, here's just one example of the countless ideas which can be found in books from the last century (and which should probably remain where they were devised):

- To keep flies off gilt picture frames, boil three or four onions in a pint of water and apply to the frames with a soft brush.

Appendix D
ONIONS FOR DYEING

Onions are not likely to be anyone's first choice for dyeing fabrics; yet onion skins, like many other vegetable substances, can be used for this purpose. As with other natural dyes, onion skins adhere best and most firmly on wool. Silk also "takes" to natural dyes. However, cotton and linen are more difficult, so the beginner should not attempt these until quite proficient. The majority of natural dyes are not permanent unless the cloth is previously impregnated with what is termed a mordant, which possesses a very strong affinity both with cloth and the dye, and therefore serves to bind the one with the other.

Red onion skins fixed with a chrome mordant turn wool and silk deep gold. Linen and cotton take on a tan or brown color from this formula. Red onion skins have also yielded a fine lime green color in certain processes. Yellow onion skins with an alum mordant impart various tones of yellows to brassy orange on wool or silk. The onion bulb itself is said to yield a lighter yellow color.

Because dyeing is a complicated and delicate process which requires considerable preparation, complete instructions for dyeing should be obtained from one of the many books on the market devoted solely to this subject. Our purpose here is to make known still another use for the onion.

The following books may be consulted for further details and instructions for dyeing with natural substances:

For brief descriptions of dye plants, *A Guide to the*

Huntington Herb Garden by John C. MacGregor. [San Marino, CA]: The Huntington Library, [1983].

For basic instructions in dyeing with plants and a listing of dye plants, *The Herbalist* by Joseph E. Meyer; revised and updated by Clarence Meyer. Glenwood, Illinois: Meyerbooks, [1991].

For a complete guide to the subject see the following books:

Dyes From Plants by Seonaid M. Robertson. New York: Van Nostrand Reinhold Company, 1973.

Dyes From Your Garden by Berenice Gillette Conner. Miami, Florida: E.A. Seemann Publishing, Inc., [1975].

Appendix E
SOURCES FOR SEEDS AND PLANTS

Many horticultural firms offer onion seeds or sets in their annual catalogs. Listed below are those firms which routinely send out free catalogs upon request. Other firms, which charge a fee for their catalogs, can be found in the advertising sections of newspapers and magazines. Firms marked by an asterisk also offer flowering ornamental onion plants.

W. Atlee Burpee and Co., Warminster, PA 18974

Cook's Garden, P.O. Box 535, Londonderry, VT 05148

*Henry Field's Seed and Nursery Co., 415 North Burnett, Shenandoah, IA 51602

*Gurney's Seed and Nursery Co., 110 Capital Street, Yankton, SD 57079

*Park Seed Co., Cokesbury Road, Greenwood, SC 29647

Otto Richter and Sons, Ltd., Goodwood, Ontario, Canada L0C 1A0

Shepherd's Garden Seeds, 30 Irene Street, Torrington, CT 06790

*Smith and Hawken, 25 Corte Madera, Mill Valley, CA 94941

BIBLIOGRAPHY
Culinary

Beckwith, Lillian. *Hebridean Cookbook*. London: Arrow Books, 1976.

Bothwell, Jean. *Onions Without Tears: A Collection of Intriguing Recipes*. New York: Hastings House, Publishers, [1950]; reprinted as *The Onion Cookbook*. New York: Dover Publications, Inc., [1976].

Brobeck, Florence. *Old-Time Pickling and Spicing Recipes*. New York: Gramercy Publishing Company, [c. 1953].

[Compilation] *Devinely Delicious Cook Book*. [No place, no publisher, 1983].

De Loup, Maximilian. *The American Salad Book*. New York: Doubleday, Page and Company, 1912.

Eliel, Lille W. *A German American Cook Book*. New York: Siegel-Cooper Co., [1897].

Grigson, Jane. *Jane Grigson's Vegetable Book*. New York: Penguin Books, [1979].

Harland, Marion. *Common Sense In The Household*. New York: Charles Scribner's Sons, 1883.

Hill, Janet McKenzie. *Practical Cooking and Serving*. New York: Doubleday, Page and Company, 1922.

Mace, Herbert. *Storing, Preserving and Pickling*. London: A. and C. Black, 1948.

Mendelsohn, Oscar A. *A Salute To Onions: Some Reflections On Cookery . . . and Cooks*. New York: Hawthorn Books, Inc., [1966].

Miller, Margaret B. *Dairymen's Country Club Cook Book*. [No place, no publisher, c. 1956].

Smith, Herman. *Stina: The Story of a Cook*. [New York:] M. Barrows and Co., Inc., 1944.

Gardening

Lerner, B. Rosie. *Onions and Their Relatives*. West Lafayette, IN: Purdue University Cooperative Extension Service, [1987].

Phillips, Roger and Martyn Rix. *The Random House Book of Bulbs*. New York: Random House, [1989].

Webster, Helen Noyes. *Herbs — How to Grow Them and How to Use Them*. Boston: Charles T. Branford Company, 1947.

Wilder, Louise Beebe. *What Happens In My Garden*. New York: The Macmillan Company, 1935.

General

Knaggs, H. Valentine. *Onions and Cress*. Fourth Edition. London: The C.W. Daniel Company, [1925].

Masefield, G.B. and M. Wallis, S.G. Harrison, B.E. Nicholson. *The Oxford Book of Food Plants*. Cambridge: Oxford University Press, 1969.

Medsger, Oliver Perry. *Edible Wild Plants*. New York: The Macmillan Company, 1939.

Spencer, Edwin Rollin. *Just Weeds*. New York: Charles Scribner's Sons, 1940.

[The United States Department of Agriculture]. *Food: The Yearbook of Agriculture 1959*. Washington, D.C.: The United States Government Printing Office, [1959].

Lore

Arber, Agnes. *Herbals: Their Origin and Evolution. A Chapter in the History of Botany 1470-1670*. Cambridge: Oxford University Press, 1912.

Dyer, T.F. Thiselton. *The Folk-Lore of Plants*. London: Chatto and Windus, 1889.

Folkard, Richard. *Plant Lore, Legends and Lyrics*. London: Sampson, Low, Marston and Company, 1892.

Friend, Rev. Hilderic. *Flowers and Flower Lore*. London: Swan Sonnenschein, LeBas and Lowrey, 1886.

Inwards, Richard. *Weather Lore: A Collection of Proverbs, Sayings, and Rules Concerning the Weather*. London: Elliot Stock, 1898.

Phillips, Henry. *The Companion For The Kitchen Garden*. New Edition. London: Henry Colburn and Richard Bentley, 1831. [2 volumes].

Skinner, Charles M. *Myths and Legends of Flowers, Trees, Fruits, and Plants in all Ages and Climes*. Philadelphia: J.B. Lippincott Company, 1911.

Verrill, A. Hyatt. *Wonder Plants and Plant Wonders*. New York: D. Appleton-Century Company, 1939.

Medical

Bardeau, Fabrice. *Die Apotheke Gottes*. Frankfurt/Main: Verlag Ullstein GmbH., 1978.

Barton, Benjamin H., F.L.S. and Thomas Castle, M.D., F.L.S. *The British Flora Medica: A History of the Medicinal Plants of Great Britain*. A New Edition, Revised, Condensed, and Partly Rewritten by John R. Jackson, A.L.S. London: Chatto and Windus, 1877.

Cromie, John D. *Oxford Medical Advisor For The Home*. New York: Oxford University Press, 1931.

Dalziel, J.M. *The Useful Plants of West Tropical Africa*. London: Crown Agents for Overseas Governments and Administrations, 1955.

Ewell, James. *The Medical Companion or Family Physician*. The Tenth Edition. Philadelphia: Thomas, Cowperthwait and Co., 1847.

Fernie, W.T., M.D. *Kitchen Physic: At Home For The Doctor And Helpful For Homely Cures*. Bristol: John Wright and Co., 1901.

Fernie. *Meals Medicinal: with "Herbal Simples" (of Edible Parts)*. Bristol: John Wright and Co., 1905.

Fernie. *Herbal Simples Approved For Modern Uses of Cure*. Bristol: John Wright and Sons Ltd., 1914.

Flach, Grete. *Aus Meinem Rezeptschatz-Kastlein*. Freiburg: Hermann Bauer Verlag KG., 1977.

Goock, Roland. *Gewürze und Kräuter von A – Z*. Berlin: Bertelsmann Ratgeberuerlag, [n.d.].

Guerrero, Leon. *Medicinal Uses of Philippine Plants*. Manila: Philippine Bureau of Forestry Bulletin, 1921.

Hertwig, Hugo. *Knaurs Heilpflanzenbuch.* Munich: Droe-mersche Verlagsanstalt Th. Knaur Nachf., 1954.

Losch, Dr. F. *Krauterbuch.* Munich: Verlag von J.F. Schrei-ber, [1924].

Martinez, Maximino. *Plantas Medicinales De Mexico.* [No place, 1969.]

Mertes, Peter. *500 Heilpflanzen.* Ravensburg: Otto Maier Verlag, [1936].

Nadkarni, Dr. K.M. *Indian Materia Medica.* Third Edition, Revised and Enlarged by A.K. Nadkani. Bombay: G.R. Bhatkal for the Popular Book Depot, 1954. [2 vol-umes].

Pereire, J. *The Elements of Materia Medica and Therapeutics.* Second American, from the Last London Edition, En-larged and Improved. Philadelphia: Lea and Blanchard, 1846. [2 volumes].

Quisumbing, Eduardo. *Medicinal Plants of the Philippines.* Manila: Bureau of Printing, 1951.

Rogler, August. *Krautersegen.* Wien-Munich: Cura Verlag, [n.d.].

Schauenberg, Paul and Ferdinand Paris. *Heilpflanzen.* Munich: BLV Verlag, 1970.

Stille, Alfred, M.D. and John Maisch, Phar. *The National Dispensatory.* Third Edition. Philadelphia: Henry C. Lea's Son & Co., 1884.

INDEX